1 MONTH OF
FREE
READING

at

www.ForgottenBooks.com

By purchasing this book you are
eligible for one month membership to
ForgottenBooks.com, giving you
unlimited access to our entire
collection of over 1,000,000 titles via
our web site and mobile apps.

To claim your free month visit:

www.forgottenbooks.com/free169023

ISBN 978-0-265-17500-2
PIBN 10169023

This book is a reproduction of an important historical work. Forgotten Books uses
state-of-the-art technology to digitally reconstruct the work, preserving the original format
whilst repairing imperfections present in the aged copy. In rare cases, an imperfection in
the original, such as a blemish or missing page, may be replicated in our edition. We do,
however, repair the vast majority of imperfections successfully; any imperfections that
remain are intentionally left to preserve the state of such historical works.

COMMITTEE ON DEATH OF PRESIDENT LINCOLN.

Hon. Mr. HARRISON.
Messrs. PRATT of Norwich,
OAKLEY of Bristol,
MERRITT of Greenwich,
PAYNE of North Haven,
AMSBURY of Killingly,
HART of Cornwall,
HUNGERFORD of East Haddam,
PAINE of Woodstock.

GENERAL ASSEMBLY,
MAY SESSION, A. D. 1865.

Resolved, That the thanks of this General Assembly are hereby tendered to the Hon. HENRY C. DEMING, for his able, eloquent and patriotic Address on the life and character of ABRAHAM LINCOLN.

Resolved, That thirty-five hundred copies of said address be printed for the use of this Assembly.

IN SENATE, June 9th, 1865.

Passed.

WM. T. ELMER, *Clerk.*

HOUSE OF REPRESENTATIVES, June 9th, 1865.

Passed.

JOHN R. BUCK, *Clerk.*

EULOGY.

By authority of a joint resolution, the Select Committee on the Death of President Lincoln, invited the Hon. Henry Champion Deming, of Hartford, Member of Congress from the First District, to deliver before the General Assembly a eulogy upon the life, character and services of the lamented President.

The invitation was accepted by the honorable gentleman, and the eulogy was delivered at Allyn Hall, in the city of Hartford, on the evening of June 8th, 1865.

The Hall was festooned with flags and mourning, and music was furnished by Colt's Band.

The meeting was called to order by Hon. H. Lynde Harrison, Senator from the Sixth District, who announced the following officers:

PRÉSIDENT.

His Excellency, WM. A. BUCKINGHAM.

VICE-PRESIDENTS.

(*On the part of the Senate.*)

Hon. ROGER AVERILL, President,   Hon. SAMUEL ROCKWELL,
  " EDWARD I. SANDFORD,   " SYLVESTER SMITH,
  " CHARLES H. MALLORY,   " JOHN T. WAITE,

6

Hon. Benjamin Pomeroy,
" Edwin H. Bugbee,
" Hrnry W. Peck,
" William E. Cone,
Hon. Charles A. Atkins.

Hon. Charles W. Ballard,
" Orlando J. Hodge,
" Robbins Battell,
" Jasper H. Bolton,

(On the part of the House.)

Hon. E. K. Foster, Speaker,
Mr H. K. W. Welch,
" Franklin Chamberlin,
" Oliver S. Williams,
" Rial Chaney,
" Charles W. Scott,
" Phineas T. Barnum,
" Samuel G. Beardsley,
" Henry Hammond,
" Charles Osgood,
" Abijah Catlin,
" Henry S. Barbour,
" Luther Boardman,
" George Kellogg,

Mr. Henry B. Harrison,
" John S. Rice,
" Harris B. Munson,
" Frederick J. Kingsbury,
" Samuel Mowry,
" David P. Nichols,
" Myron L. Mason,
" Edward L. Cundall,
" David Gallup,
" David E. Bostwick,
" Andrew B. Mygatt,
" William G. Coe,
" William R. Clark,
" Julius Converse.

SECRETARIES,

(On the part of the Senate.)

Hon. Frederick W. Russell,   Hon. Francis A. Sanford.

(On the part of the House)

Mr. Samuel J. Day,
" Alonzo F. Wood,
" F. St. John Lockwood,
" Oscar Tourtelotte,
" George M. Woodruff,
" John M. Douglas,

Mr. Edward S. Scranton,
" Albert L. Avery,
" Apollos Comstock,
" Lucian Carpenter,
" Lewis Catlin,
" George D. Hastings.

On taking the chair, Governor Buckingham was loudly applauded. He said:

LADIES AND GENTLEMEN :—

It is difficult for us to review the past and contemplate the rapid and marvelous changes which have crowded the events of generations into a few passing months, without inquiring whether it all has not been a dream; and yet our minds and hands have been so much occupied, and our hearts so deeply affected by the scenes through which we have passed, that our judgment and consciousness decide the question, and assure us that we have not been moved by visions and dreams, but by realities.

The rebellion has been a reality. The power of the government has not been imaginary. The organization of armies, their conflict upon a thousand battle-fields, the overthrow of our national enemies, the suppression of the rebellion, and the emancipation of the enslaved, are all real events, which have surprised ourselves and astonished the civilized world. But events alone do not make history. It is read in the character and lives of those who have been active participators in the scenes which have transpired. There can be no correct history of the Israelites, of their oppression and deliverence, of their passage through the sea and through the wilderness, without the lives of

Moses and Joshua. There can be no true history of the twenty-five years of European war, commencing with the French revolution and ending with the battle of Waterloo, without the life of Napoleon. Nor can there be a correct history of this nation, as it has passed through this great struggle for existence, without the life of Abraham Lincoln, and without connecting his name with that immortal proclamation which gave freedom and manhood to four millions of bondmen.

The General Assembly has properly invited a gentleman of distinguished ability, who was intimately acquainted with Mr. Lincoln, to present to us this evening, and to weave into our nation's history, the life and character of our late President, so that all may see those qualities of heart and mind by which he endeared himself to the people, and which stamped his official acts with a purity and patriotism which command universal respect and admiration. No one can draw his character in lines of more distinctness and accuracy, or present it in more attractive and life-like colors, or show more clearly the precise influence which he exerted over public affairs during this period of danger, than the orator of the evening, whom I now introduce—the Hon. Henry C. Deming.

Mr. Deming was received with long continued applause.   He said :

MAY IT PLEASE YOUR EXCELLENCY, AND GENTLEMEN OF THE GENERAL ASSEMBLY :—

FROM the seat of our Republican Empire which, during the last four years and for all coming time, he has preserved from the spoiler by his wisdom and address; through avenues of weeping myriads who have thronged the thoroughfare, all the way from the Potomac to the prairie, to look on his bier, bear his pall, and to scatter on his casket the fragrant offerings of affection ; through great commonwealths which, with all the pomp and circumstance of mournful state, have received him on their threshold and attended him, with uncovered heads, and with every oblation of sorrow from border to border ; through magnificent cities draped from cornice to basement in all the emblems and wailing with every motto and articulation of woe; to the sighing of the air, over the groaning earth ; to the booming of minute gun, to muffled drum and the plaintive burst of martial music ; to dirge, anthem and lamentation, ABRAHAM LINCOLN has reached that silent home of all the living, which " buries every error, covers every defect, extinguishes every resentment."

After life's fitful fever he sleeps well,
Treason has done his worst, nor steel nor poison,
Malice domestic, foreign levy, nothing
Can touch him further!

With ampler honors, and with more of the symbols and ceremonial of universal love and veneration, than this continent ever paid before to any of her sons, the funeral pageant had scarcely reached the portals of the tomb, before the posthumous tributes of another Hemisphere are borne across the Ocean. The suffering of her eldest born fairly melts into sympathy the estranged heart of our haughty Island Mother, and England mourns, as when Nelson expired in the arms of victory, or as when the gates of her Great Abbey, closed upon the ashes of the greatest of her warriors. The generous Queen draws upon her own inconsolable domestic grief, for consolation to a wife and mother, like herself bereaved, and pens with her own royal hand a letter of condolence. The brazen lips of the impassive Emperor break their grim silence to utter sententious panegyric. From the mountains of Switzerland, which have for centuries broken the waves of oppression, we have free, generous, intelligent homage to a LIBERATOR, whom William Tell would have been proud to recognize as a brother. Ancient cities, which might have wept, when at the base of Pompey's statue great Cæsar fell, have, by their representatives, hung in all the trappings of grief the august Hall, wherein they are now legislating for regenerated Italy. The free towns and corporate guilds of Netherlands and Germany, which wrung their charters from Charles the Bold, and rocked European freedom in its cradle, vie with each other in canonizing a child of the people, who leads the Great Republic from darkness and bondage, to light and liberty. The Prussian Chamber of Deputies, receive with enthusiastic applause, the eloquent eulogium of a personal acquaintance of the PRESIDENT, and affirm a most earnest resolution of respect by unanimously rising from their seats, in token of superlative courtesy, and the Lower House of the Austrian Reichsrath which conducts its stately proceedings, according to forms and usages handed down from the Feudal Ages, is as wild and demonstrative, upon the receipt of the sad intelligence, as an Indignation Meeting of Loyal Leagues in Union Square. Indeed, for ABRAHAM LINCOLN one cry of universal regret is raised all over the civilized earth.

It is difficult to descend from the fervor of these first impassioned outbursts of a world wide grief, to cool analysis and historic delineation. And yet that is the task before me. I should violate the proprieties of this occasion, if I indulged in mere rhapsodies, however grand and well deserved, for I am to present an estimate of character to a Legislative body, and I can not forget that it habitually dwells in the mild atmosphere congenial to deliberation, that it solicits unvarnished statement instead of rhetorical flourish, and records its own judgment in the composed style of fact and argument.

In these days of photographs, it is almost superfluous to paint in speech the portrait of a distinguished man, but as the resources of the language have been exhausted in depreciation of MR. LINCOLN's person, I am unwilling that he shall pass into history, in any shape, which may repel the enthusiasm due by posterity, to exalted merit and heroic achievement. Let us at all events place on record the image which he really wore that he may not descend the ages according to malicious caricature. MR. LINCOLN's person was not one to move their applause, to whom an Apollo or an Antinous are the only ideals of physical humanity, or whose undeviating types of manliness are found on the canvas of a Reynolds or a Stuart, but it was not uninteresting for those to contemplate who regard the human form and face, as a veritable record of life's experiences, and to some extent, an index of character. It was not unsuited to one who was born from a rude stock, in a wild forest, and was nurtured and moulded by

constant warfare, with wilderness life, and iron fortune, and frontier hardships. Conceive a tall and
gaunt figure, more than six feet in height, not only
unencumbered with superfluous flesh, but reduced
to the minimum working standard of cord, and sinew,
and muscle, strong and indurated by exposure and
toil, with legs and arms long and attenuated, but
not disproportionately so to the long and attenuated
trunk ; in posture and carriage not ungraceful, but
with the grace of unstudied and careless ease, rather
than of cultivated airs and high-bred pretensions.
His dress is uniformly of black throughout, and
would attract but little attention in a well dressed
circle, if it hung less loosely upon him and the
ample white shirt collar was not turned over his
cravat in the western style. The face that sur-
mounts this figure is half Roman and half Indian,
bronzed by climate, furrowed by life struggles,
seamed with humor, the head is massive and covered
with dark, thick and unmanageable hair, the brow
is wide and well developed, the nose large and
fleshy, the lips full, cheeks thin, and drawn down in
strong corded lines, which, but for the wiry whiskers,
would disclose the machinery which moves the broad
jaw. The eyes are dark gray, sunk in deep sockets,
but bright, soft and beautiful in expression, and
sometimes lost and half abstracted, as if their glance

was reversed and turued inward, or as if the soul
which lighted them was far away. The teeth are
white and regular, and it is only when a smile, radi-
ant, captivating and winning as was ever given to
mortal, transfigures the plain countenance, that you
begin to realize that it is not impossible for artists to
admire and woman to love it.

As the world has rung with ridicule of the ungain-
liness of his manners, I may be permitted to say, that
without any pretensions to superfine polish, they
were frank, cordial, and dignified, without rudeness,
without offence, and without any violation of the
proprieties and etiquettes of his high position. As
fastidious and keen a master of such nice matters as
Mr. Everett has said, "I recognize in the PRESIDENT, a
full measure of the qualities which entitle him to the
personal respect of the people. On the only social
occasion on which I ever had the honor to be in his
company, viz: the Commemoration at Gettysburg,
he sat at the table at the house of my friend David
Willis, Esq., by the side of several distinguished per-
sons, ladies and gentlemen, foreigners and Americans,
among them the French Minister at Washington,
since appointed French Ambassador at Madrid, and
the Admiral of the French Fleet, and that in gentle-
manly appearance, manners and conversation he was
the peer of any man at the table."

To borrow one of his own conversational phrases he did'nt brag on deportment. He was not a Turveydrop or Sir Harcourt Courtly or General Banks. It would have puzzled him to stand in tableau for the Earl of Chatham, or the Pompeian Ajax. He was not proud of his leg, like President Dwight, nor was he a George the Fourth at a bow. He stood, and moved, and bowed, without affectation, and without obtrusive awkwardness, pretty much as nature prompted, and as if he regarded *carriage* as about as bad a criterion as *color* of genuine nobility of soul. He was not overcareful of his dignity, feeling assured that his dignity could take care of itself, and consenting to rend the web of official formalities, and to waive all ceremony and precedence which might bar his passage to a good deed by the most expeditious route. He has been convicted in contempt of " the divinity which doth hedge a king," of conferring with his counsellors in a great emergency, and of performing an act of kindness and mercy, enveloped in no robe of state but a cotton nightgown of scanty pattern, and on one memorable occasion he even presumed to solve an enigma, raised in a congress of ambassadors, by the little story of " root hog or die." He was what Dr. Johnson calls a thoroughly "clubbable" man, eminently social and familiar; in private interviews and sometimes in public, overflowing with illustrations of every theme, always apt and racy, and frequently humorous, with a habit like the Doctor himself, of upsetting a pedantry or a sophism by an epigram or an anecdote, and with a story telling method of reasoning like our own Doctor Franklin. While unrivaled as a *raconteur* in the pith and variety of his store, he was not half so broad in his narratives as many an assuming Chesterfield on both sides of the water. It is the weak invention of false friends and open enemies, to lay at his door all the prurient jokes which their foul imaginations conceived and to falsely asseverate that he was in the habit of indulging in unseemly jest and repartee on grave and solemn occasions. I can adopt and endorse the precise language of Mr. F. B. Carpenter, who as an artist had free access to MR. LINCOLN's presence, and was for several months an inmate of the White House, when he says, " I feel that it is due to Mr. Lincoln's memory to state, that during my residence in Washington, after witnessing his intercourse with all classes of people, including Governors, Senators, Members of Congress, Officers of the Army and familiar friends, I can not recollect to have heard him relate a circumstance to any one of them all that would have been out of place if uttered in a lady's drawing room. I am aware that a different impression may prevail, founded it may be in some instances on facts, but where there is one fact of the kind, I am persuaded that there are forty falsehoods at least."

Of his intellectual capacity, Mr. Lincoln gave the most signal proof, in that memorable contest with Judge Douglas, and his speeches are in no sense inferior to his rivals—the Charles James Fox of our forum, by universal consent the most athletic and expert off-hand debater who ever graced the United States Senate. The PRESIDENT'S mind was so original and self dependent, so unwilling to borrow knowledge and opinion, that he fairly scorned all adventitious support and external auxiliaries. No President ever leaned so lightly upon his Cabinet. No man reproduces less in official documents, the argument and thought which he imbibes at consultations, and it is a marvelous fact that no sentence is to be found in any of his state papers, which suggests the suspicion of any other impress but that of his own mint, or where he attempts to strengthen or vindicate a position, by quoting from any book or citing any authority. And his greatness, his greatness! is the most original and *bizarre* in the world's history, shaped after no model, suggesting as a compact whole no pattern, no parallel—not even a resemblance, contravening every antique and modern standard of Hero-worship,—a greatness which admits of no exact analysis and can only be loosely described as composed of great simplicity, great naturalness, great bonhomie, great shrewdness, great strength, great devotion, great equanimity, and great success, on the greatest theatre ever offered to such qualities for exhibition. He appears like an erratic streaming comet amid the fixed orbs of greatness, a fiery meteor plunging and howling through their subdued and chastened atmosphere. Ennobled by no patent but that of nature, with no diploma but his record; crowned, as it were, with the wild flowers of the forest and with all its flavor and freshness upon him, he walks into the surprised Pantheon of the world's great men, a huge, grotesque Backwoodsman, but with credentials to admission which can not be challenged or disallowed; like the hirsute and half naked Brennus striding into the grave and reverend decorums of a Roman Senate; like Hans Luther's plebeian and beetle-browed son confronting the stoled, mitered and ermined Diet of Charles the Fifth; like a red-nosed, cropped and mail-clad Cromwell shuffling through the silken splendors, the Vandyke dresses, the perfumed love-locks, and the fastidious etiquette of outraged Whitehall; like St. Artegans' iron soldier marching, with his invincible flail, into the startled and shrinking ranks of vulnerable and pain suffering warriors. It may be said of him, as has been said of another indigenous American type of manliness, that he taught the world " a new idea of greatness." It is somewhat surprising that with all his superabundance of wit and humor, he was but frugally endowed with imagination and fancy, without wing for the air, with not even enough like the ostrich to aid him along the earth. He never uses a figure of speech to decorate or enliven his style, and but seldom for the purpose of illustrating a thought or exposing a fallacy. He contemned all the elegancies of diction, using only plain homespun English, aiming at direct and compact statement in the fewest words, and those sometimes chosen with more respect to convenience than precision.

His education was self-acquired and unpretending, and, in the department of History, wherein the Past by experience and example instructs and exhorts the Present, and therefore so essential to genuine statesmanship, it was somewhat narrow and defective. It must be constantly borne in mind, that a superlative kindness and a disposition to oblige everybody, were fairly autocratic in him, sometimes holding in complete subjection all the other powers and forces of his nature, and frequently controlling, against their protest, his opinions and actions. "I have never willingly planted a thorn in any man's bosom," is the accurate description which he gives of himself. The domination of this amiable disposition must be constantly remembered, and carried along with you into the development and estimate of his public career, which I am attempting to present.

The chief mental equipments which he brought to the mighty task before him, were that downright uncompromising common sense which seems to divine its way through the most intricate problems, a keen insight into human nature, an intimate acquaintance with the spasmodic movements of the American mind, a natural aptitude, improved by professional discipline, in chaining premise to conclusion, and in detecting the occult relations of political cause to political effect, great caution in forming opinions, honesty and sincerity of purpose, inflexible persistence in what he regarded as public duty, and a conscientious sense of his responsibility to the country and to mankind. He had a temper habitually cheerful, but not, as some have falsely assumed, inflexibly so, for in my brief acquaintance with it, I have seen it wear every shade from exultation to despair. Laughter in abundance was in him but tears were also there. To these characteristics should always be added, an intuitive comprehension of the precise line which divides Right from Wrong, and implicit reliance upon the goodness and wisdom of Almighty God.

Let us now see how this peculiar organization

addressed itself to the tremendous task which he has just triumphantly achieved. And what a creative task it was? Armies, navies, cash, credit, opinion, all to be created, heroism to be evolved from money-making thrift, pluck from pusilanimity, steadfast principle from vacillating expediency, constancy and endurance from over-sanguine and vain-glorious dreams—and millions of self-willed and arrogant despots to be humbled forever. He began by almost re-creating himself.

In one of the brief speeches which ABRAHAM LIN-COLN made, when as President elect, and in the full flush of life, he traveled the same road upon which he has recently returned, in the habiliments of the grave, he says to his countrymen: "In my view of the present aspect of affairs, there need be no bloodshed or war. There is no necessity for it. I am not in favor of such a course, and I may say in advance that there will be no bloodshed unless it be forced upon the government, and then it will be compelled to act in self-defence." This brief sentence furnishes us with the first insight into his mind, when contemplating the task before him, and it unlocks all the mystery and explains the purely defensive course of his administration, during the first two months of its existence.

At the same time Jefferson Davis, on his progress

to Montgomery, to install a hostile government, thus proclaims his setiments:—" The time for compromise has passed, and we are now determined to maintain our position, and make all who oppose us smell southern gunpowder and feel southern steel." And this short utterance epitomizes the spirit and temper of the Chief Conspirator, when he was commencing the despotic reign which has just been so ignominiously closed by Col. Pritchard at Irwinsville. By the light of events we now learn, what was not surmised by the most sagacious at the time, that the Rebellion was all armed, equipped, in line of battle and thirsting for the sanguinary fray, before the future Conqueror of the Rebellion had convinced himself that any blood would be shed, or had systematised any plan of counteracting the revolutionary agencies, which were threatening his own and the nation's life. So far, however, from regarding the hesitancy of the PRESIDENT at the outset, to avow any radical or even any methodized policy, of dealing with the rebellion, as proof of imbecility, I accept it as conclusive evidence of genuine greatness and strength. He was ignorant of its implacable determination like every other man guileless of complicity with it, and a premature radical policy would have subjected him instantly, to the reproach from a vast majority of his countrymen, of stimulating an undeveloped and embryo crime, which conciliation and caution might strangle ; and *any* policy, while the insurrection was unorganized, would have clearly convicted him .of the hollowness and insincerity of the mere pretender. It would have implied superhuman prevision, sublime conceit, or arrant quackery. He was about assuming the helm of Government, when the tempest was abroad in its fury, when every headland was buried in storm and darkness, when every Pharos as well as the eternal lights of Heaven were extinguished, when the needle was no longer true to the pole, when all prognostics failed, when all charts and tables of previous navigators were at fault, and the laboring ship must be steered over the wide and pathless ocean by conjecture alone. This was no time for laying out her bearings and course for a four years' voyage, and our wise and truthful PILOT, avowing manfully his infirmity, in such an unparalleled tornado, and reverently invoking divine guidance, prudently abstained, during that memorable progress, from committing himself to any rigid and inflexible theory, which would prevent him afterwards, from adapting his measures to the growth and development of the monstrous anomaly, and of justifying his policy by its frighful vicissitudes and crime.

Nor is the language of his Inaugural much more decisive. His temper and spirit towards it is most

24

forbearing and admirable. He is not yet authorized to treat it as a maniac, and therefore addresses it as a perverse but accountable creature. So far as the Rebellion had evinced its character and intentions, just so far his plan of dealing with it was therein frankly and unmistakably announced. It undertook to vindicate its revolutionary attitude, by pretending to fear an unauthorized destruction of Slavery in the States, and the new PRESIDENT, as in duty bound, in his first official address disclaimed for himself and his supporters any such purpose, both by a full and pointed denial, and by ample citation of the antecedent and recorded declarations of the Republican party and its Chief. In prosecution of its purposes the rebellion had already seized Forts, Navy Yards, Custom Houses, Arsenals, and had prohibited the collection of duties, and he calmly but decisively declares, that "the power confided to him will be used, to hold, occupy and possess the property and places belonging to the Government, and to collect the duties and imports." And that this might not seem too threatening a declaration, he adds the important qualification, that " beyond what may be necessary for these objects, there will be no invasion, no using of force against or among the people anywhere." In deference to the irritation which prevailed in the insurrectionary

States, he expressly foregoes the right of appointing obnoxious strangers to Federal offices within their limits, and promises that the mails shall be furnished to all parts of the Union, until they are violently repelled.

In this brief statement, I have condensed all the foreshadowings of a policy, which this wise and unfaltering PRESIDENT vouchsafed to the world, when consciously entering upon the most perilous era of our history, and assuming the most momentous responsibilities. While we have in it but one sentence, which even the over-sensitive chivalry could construe into a menace, we are prodigally furnished with conciliatory promises, and with such winning arguments and admonitions only, as a tender father might employ with a wayward offspring. Up to the time when he took the oath of office upon the eastern portico of the Capitol, he had pushed forbearance beyond the point where it ceases to be a virtue, and it is perfectly apparent that it had not yet dawned upon him, that his hand was soon to wield a scourge, terrible enough to chastise two God-defying centuries of crime, or that his chief mission to this earth was to conduct a nation through the jaws of death and the gates of hell, to regenerated and immortal life.

Let me now attempt to ascertain, at what precise

period he abandoned this preconceived and cherished idea of compromising the embroilment by a mere warlike demonstration, and let me also attempt to analyze the difficulties, which, a resolution in favor of uncompromising and aggressive hostilities, encounters from his conservative habits, from his peculiar emotional and intellectual organization, and reproduce, as far as I am able, the arguments, which persuaded his placable and scrupulous mind to the unhesitating and implacable purpose of exercising all the tremendous powers conferred upon him by the Rights of War, and of grasping every weapon in its terrible arsenal.

The Time, when this decided change in his purpose first appears, was more than a month after our flag was struck from Sumpter's crumbling battlements, more than a month after that bugle blast which summoned seventy-five thousand men to arms, a month at least after the bloody baptism of Massachusetts troops in the streets of Baltimore. We have his own authentic manifestoes to demonstrate, that as late as the first of May, 1861, he had not abandoned temporizing expedients, and we learn by evidence equally conclusive, that before the month had closed, he had finally resolved to turn upon the inveterate Rebellion the unbridled wrath of War. The hour, when doubt and hesitancy first yielded to

the stern command of remorseless duty, must have
been the soberest, saddest, solemnest of his faithful
life, not from doubt of the result, though that was
sufficiently perplexing; not from fear of the consequences, though these were appalling enough; not
from the weight of responsibility, though that might
have staggered the most unyielding determination,
but it was sad and solemn, because ABRAHAM LINCOLN,
above and beyond all other men, loved Peace and
hated War; because seiges, battles, strife, swords,
bayonets, rifles, cannon, all the paraphernalia and
instruments of brute force, were abhorrent to his
enlightened and benevolent nature. Shall we raise
the latch, and enter in to the secret chamber of that
capacious and genial soul, when this fell resolve was
first reached, when the frightful vision of War, in all
its terrors clad, supplants there the hope of conciliation and the dream of peace? I speak, what I heard
from his own lips when I say, that it was reached
after sleepless nights, after a severe conflict with
himself, and with extreme reluctance. By a strange
and cruel freak of fate, the duty of waging the
bloodiest war in history was imposed upon the most
peace loving and amiable ruler in all time, upon a
man whose maxim was (in the language of one of
his favorite texts,) "let the potsherd strive with the
potsherds of the Earth"—and into whose mind, had

been thoroughly ingrained that traditional notion of our politics, that the first drop of blood, shed in a sectional strife, was the death-knell of the American Union.

Let us enter in, where that now disembodied spirit was, in the recesses of its clay tenement, in stormy debate with itself. What throes, what agony do we witness! What heart rending sobs, what heaven piercing prayers that the cup may pass from his lips! Here was that conservative mind, trained to habits of professional caution, with the strongest bias towards legality and moderation, which had uniformly steered itself by the certain lights of jurisprudence, which had invoked no remedies but the peaceful ones of the Courts, the Constitution and the Law, which had never combated Error but with reason and persuasion alone, and had abjured the ordeal of battle and the arbitrament of force, as obsolete and heathenish enormities. Here are all these mature, earnest opinions and prepossessions, all dominant from fifty years of undisputed sway, wrestling impotently with the War ideas and the overmastering War Revelation of yesterday. What an unwelcome intruder the conviction is to the serene virtues, which had hitherto exclusively occupied this holy sanctuary. Domesticated here are Justice and Mercy, ("and earthly power is likest God's when Mercy seasons Justice.")

Justice and Mercy, which hold the balances quite evenly, but the hair's weight which oscillates them, uniformly found in Mercy's scale, and how repulsive it is to these righteous and discriminating attributes, to let loose upon the people a wild and furious Avenger that devours alike innocence and guilt? Here too dwell sensibilities and affections so acute, that they fling wide open the doors of the soul to every one who approaches in Misfortune's name, grant the prayer of Sorrow before it is half uttered, and which the small inarticulate wail of infancy instantly melts into tears of most compassionate tenderness; how are these sensitive fibers wrung and tortured when it suddenly flashes upon them, that the loving hand which has only learned to soothe and relieve the miserable, is commissioned by inexorable fate, to break the fourth seal of the Apocalypse, and, "behold a pale horse! and his name who sat on him was Death and Hell followed him; and power was given unto them over the fourth part of the earth, to kill with the sword and with hunger and with Death and with the beasts of the earth." Movelessly, movelessly rooted also in this great heart, is a superfine sense of humor, craving hilarity and harmless mirth, and joy-inspiring wit and anecdote, as the only effectual relief to an over anxious spirit and an over-tasked brain, and how reluctantly does this part of his nature admit to close companionship, the gloomy forebodings, the bitter memories, the dreadful uncertainties, the everlasting shrieks, dirges, vengeful tragedies, and heart-rending atrocities of War.

In addition to the protest of these conservative habits, and amiable emotions, upon his adoption of any radical and thorough-going policy of grappling with the Rebellion, he was also, like many others, held back for a season, by the legal scruples which his reflecting faculties were constantly suggesting. "Beset," as it has been well said, "by fanatics of principle, on one side, who would give no heed to the limitations of his written authority, and by fanatics of party, on the other, who were not only deaf to the obligations of justice, but would hear of no policy large enough for a revolutionary emergency, Mr. Lincoln never forgot, for an instant, that he was a constitutional ruler." The Constitution of the United States which it takes but twenty minutes to read, can be studied for twice twenty years, without exhausting its meaning, or comprehending its vast treasury of express and implied power. Like most of our statesmen the attention of the President, had been exclusively turned to the Peace side of the instrument, to the provisions which address themselves to conditions of unbroken amity, domestic tranquility,

to the preservation of amicable relations between the
States, and to the development, under their auspices,
of commerce, industry, manufactures and trade.
The powers it grants over internal improvements,
over foreign and inter-State commerce, currency,
duties and imposts, territories, naturalization, taxation,
bankruptcy, as well as the extent of constitutional
limitations upon the General Government, and of
constitutional prohibitions upon the States, have not
only been subjects of constant individual study, but
have been illustrated and defined, by a long, lumin-
ous and comprehensive series of judicial determina-
tions, which have the same authority and validity as
if they were incorporated into the Constitution itself.
We can all see, at a glance, how greatly these inves-
tigations and decisions have contributed to consoli-
date the Union and to enlarge and strengthen the
influence of the National government.   But Courts
and individuals have alike ignored the WAR side of
the Constitution, or drawn but feebly upon that
slumbering element in our system, which holds each
revolving planet in complete subjection to the sun.

What are its powers over States which abjure
allegiance, and conspire together for its destruction
and overthrow, and raise armies, and wage War
against it, was, fortunately, a question which no
judicial tribunal had been called upon to adjudi-

cate, which no curious theorizer had even mooted, and which Mr. Lincoln himself for the first time investigated in the third month of his administration —that parturiant and groaning May. He then concentrated his attention upon the War powers of our organic law, and found in this *terra incognita*, unexpected resources which never yet had contributed to the weight, and vigor, and terror of the Federal arm. The elements of strength and power which were hid away, in the weighty clauses, which give to the President and Congress the issues of Peace and War, were dragged to light and employed for the salvation of the Republic.

By the middle of May the doubt and haze which had settled upon the legal relation of the Insurgent States to the Government, began to disappear. On the sixth of that month, the Confederate Congress at Montgomery, declared war against the United States, and Mr. Lincoln's position, at this time, towards the gigantic peril which threatened our national existence, was described with legal exactness and accuracy, when it was said to him by an eminent civilian—"If the whole unvarnished truth is told you, sir, you are confronted by a *de facto* Rebellion, and a *de facto* War, and you are justified in treating it as the one, as the other, and as both." With equal truth it was shortly afterwards said, in the United States Senate, "it is a Rebellion swollen to the proportions of a War, and it is a War deriving its life from Rebellion. It is no less of a Rebellion because of its full blown grandeur, nor is it less a War because of the traitorous source from whence it draws its life." What are my constitutional resources against this new, strange, and double headed monster? was the first question which MR. LINCOLN put to himself, and this question, grave, severe, and momentous as was ever submitted to human arbitrament, he was called upon, without precedent, without authority, and from his habits of mind without assistance, forthwith to determine by his peculiar process of divination.

The Constitution, does it not? establishes in law and in fact, an independent government. By that act alone, all the belligerent rights, which from time immemorial, by international law belong to independent governments, were instantly conveyed to the new born nation. Yes, yes, they were all ours by the title which secured us a place in the family of nations. In abeyance during peace, they instantly vest with the first act of War, and with full grown vehemence and power surrender themselves to execute our behests, against all of our public enemies whether they rally under the bastard banner of an Insurgent State, or the legitimate flag of a recognized nation.

But not only did Mr. Lincoln find full belligerent rights, according to the laws and usages of nations, and against all armed foes, implied in the independent government which the Constitution creates and endows with the powers of self-defence, but he found, also, that they all directly and necessarily flow from the express provisions of the instrument. What is War? oh doubting Didymus! According to the books, it is "contention by force for the purpose of paralyzing an enemy." Congress has power, has it not? "to declare war," and what is this but lifting the gate and opening the sluiceway which sets in motion all the legitimate machinery which is required to paralyze an enemy? Congress has power, has it not? "to grant letters of marque and reprisal"; and what is this but commissioning two of the peculiar agencies of war, to follow the property of the enemy wherever it flees, for the purpose of punishing and impoverishing him. Congress has power "to make rules concerning captures on land and water," and what is this but providing directly for the exercise of seizure, forfeiture, contribution, confiscation, liberation. In the power conferred upon Congress, "to raise and support armies," "to provide and maintain a navy," "to make rules for the government of the land and naval forces," "to provide for the calling forth of the militia, to execute the laws of the Union, suppress insurrection and repel invasions," and, in the clinching and decisive clause which empowers it " to make all laws necessary and proper" for carrying these enumerated powers into execution, he found plenary authority for employing, in its extremest rigor, every right of war against rebels in arms.

Turning away then, from the pages of the Constitution which confer *belligerent rights*, he reperused the article which deals with Rebellion *as a crime*, and provides for it a *criminal* punishment, to be enforced in the Courts, by the peaceful processes of the *municipal* law; and he finds that levying war against the United States and adhering to their enemies is *treason*, and is liable to all the pains, penalties and forfeitures which are visited upon that *crime*.

From this long review, MR. LINCOLN rose with the conviction, that for the overthrow of the rebels he might draw upon two fountains, and a double source of power, *the Constitution* and the *rights of war ;* that as *criminals* he might pursue them by the slow and guarded processes of the first, but that as *enemies*, he could wither them with all the dread agencies and summary vengeance of the last, and he rose, too, with the full determination from which he never afterwards deflected, to draw upon both magazines, to fight from both batteries, and with all their thunder.

The powers thus claimed, are all indubitably conferred, and may be all unquestionably used, unless in behalf of rebels in arms, you urge the preposterous plea that they are not *enemies* because they are *traitors*, thereby constituting broken faith, violated oaths, and avowed treason, titles to immunity from the penalties of war, and thus disfranchise an independent nation of every belligerent right against those foes, who have once owed it allegiance, and to the guilt of treason have added that of unjust war.

If, in addition to the considerations I have urged in favor of these positions, time would permit me to cite the judgments of the Supreme Court, I could present precise points, raised in admiralty appeals, and ruled by such judges as Marshall, Livingstone, Tilghman, Taney, Grier and Nelson, which establish the principle, that the United States engaged in suppressing an insurrection of its citizens, may with entire consistency treat them as *criminals*, as *enemies*, and as *both*, and may, with equal consistency, also act in the two-fold capacity of *sovereign* and *belligerent*, according to the several measures resorted to for the accomplishment of its purpose. By inflicting, through its agent the Judiciary, the penalty which the law affixes to the capital crimes of treason and piracy, it treats them as *criminals*, and acts in its capacity as a *sovereign*, and its courts are but enforcing its *municipal* regulations. By instituting a blockade of the ports of its rebellious citizens, invading their territory, sequestrating their property, and emancipating their slaves, the Government treats them as *enemies*, and exercises its rights as a *belligerent*, and its courts, in their adjudication upon capture, seizures, and forfeitures, are organized as courts of prize, under the *law of nations*.*

I have dwelt longer, than may be deemed judicious by some, upon the process by which ABRAHAM LINCOLN's mind was gradually led, from vague and undefined notions, to defined and accurate views of the relations of the armed insurgent to the Federal Government, because it lies at the very root of his Administration of the War, because it vindicates his Constitutional fidelity, because, just as the future forest once lay in the acorn's cup, just as the full grown Rebellion once lay, in the pestilent heresy of Calhoun, just so clearly and conspicuously its inevitable death lay, in the fundamental and germinant idea, that as *criminals* they were subject to all the penalties of the Constitution, and as *enemies* to all the legal consequences of War.

In that classic drama, which first revealed to the world the masterly genius of Talford, unhappy Ion

---

* Upton's Maritime Warfare and Prize, p. 212.

proceeds upon the task, to which he was called by the audible voice of the gods, with a firm hand and unfaltering will, but with supreme pity and tenderness towards the father he was doomed to slay. With as compassionate a heart, with as complete exemption from all vengeful passions, but with as unswerving and constant a determination, this gentle PRESIDENT now dedicates his arm to the destruction of the Rebellion. And from this time forward all vascillation, compunction, and even debate, apparently disappear from his mind, as if he had accepted and surrendered himself to a vengeful destiny, or as if he regarded himself as the mere instrument of working out a great cause, which he was constrained to recognize, but powerless to control. Forthwith, rise like exhalations that impregnable cordon of earthworks in which Washington has securely reposed, forthwith the guns of Fort McHenry, and the broadside of a man of war admonish the Plug Uglies of Baltimore, that the main thoroughfare to the Capital must hereafter be inviolate, forthwith the Ohio contingent is ordered to sweep every hostile banner from the mountain fastnesses of West Virginia, forthwith Butler, from Fortress Monroe, hurls a forlorn hope against the counterscarps of Big Bethel, forthwith the tented villages disappear, like snow flakes, from the surrounding fields of the Metropolis, and the rumbling of artillery waggons upon every bridge, and the long lines of glittering bayonets which reflect the waters of the Potomac, proclaim that the Rubicon is passed, and the sacred soil invaded, forthwith, in his first message, he informs Congress, that "he has invoked the War power," and calls for four hundred thousand men and four hundred millions of dollars, that "the conflict may be short and decisive," and when it passes the Non-Intercourse Act, the Confiscation Act, the Suspension of the Habeas Corpus, they are forthwith approved, for in determining that the Government was endowed, in time of War, with unabridged belligerent rights, he had settled a principle which underlies all these controverted measures.

In the seven months which follow, he evinces an administrative vigor that would have satisfied Napoleon the Great, but it was all alas! counteracted, by a military imbecility in his Generals that was fairly sublime. It is the era of almost unrelieved disaster, commencing with the ineffaceable disgrace of Bull Run and terminating only with the capture of Fort Donelson, which first introduced to the country an immortal name, and initiated a career which has steadily marched on from victory to victory, and from Alp to Alp, up to the crowning summit of military grandeur, where Ulysses S. Grant now stands unchallenged and secure.

How nobly the PRESIDENT bore himself, during this interval of darkness that could be felt, when bold men trembled at every click of the telegraph, let two tributes offered by unfriendly voices to his Stoicism attest: the first, is from no less a master of it than Napoleon the Third, who epigramatically says: "MR. LINCOLN's highest claim upon my admiration, is a Roman equanimity, which has been tried by both extremes of fortune and disturbed by neither;" the second, is from a hostile Englishman who says, that "tried by years of failure, without achieving one great success, he not only never yielded to despondency or anger, but what is most marvellous, continually grew in self-possession and magnanimity." I once myself ventured to ask the PRESIDENT, if he had ever despaired of the country? and he told me, that "when the Peninsular Campaign terminated suddenly at Harrison's Landing, I was as nearly inconsolable as I could be and live." In the same connection I inquired, if there had ever been a period in which he thought that better management, upon the part of his Commanding General, might have terminated the War? and he answered that there were three, that the first was at Malvern Hill, where McClellan failed to command an immediate advance upon Richmond, that the second was at Chancellorville, where Hooker failed to reinforce

Sedgwick, after hearing his cannon upon the extreme right, and that the third was after Lee's retreat from Gettysburg, when Meade failed to attack him in the bend of the Potomac. After this commentary I waited for an outburst of denunciation, for a criticism at least upon the delinquent officers, but I waited in vain; so far from a word of censure escaping his lips, he soon added, that his first remark might not appear uncharitable, "I do not know that I could have given different orders had I been with them myself; I have not fully made up my mind how I should behave, when minnie balls were whistling and these great oblong shells shrieking in my ear. I might run away." The interview, which I am recalling, was last summer, just after Gen. Fremont had declined to run against him for the Presidency. The magnificent Bible, which the negroes of Washington had just presented him, lay upon the table, and while we were both examining it, I recited the somewhat remarkable passage from the Chronicles; "Eastward were six Levites, northward four a day, southward four a day and towards Assuppim two and two, at Parbar westward, four at the causeway and two at Parbar." He immediately challenged me to find any such passage as that in *his* Bible. After I had pointed it out to him, and he was satisfied of its genuineness, he asked me if I remembered the text which his friends had recently applied to Fremont, and instantly turned to a verse in the first of Samuel, put on his spectacles, and read in his slow, peculiar and waggish tone,—"And every one that was in distress, and every one that was in debt, and every one that was discontented gathered themselves unto him; and he became a Captain over them: and there were with him about four hundred men." I am here reminded of an impressive remark, which he made to me upon another occasion and which I shall never forget. He said, he had never united himself to any church, because he found difficulty in giving his assent, without mental reservation, to the long complicated statements of Christian doctrine, which characterize their Articles of belief and Confessions of Faith. "When any church," he continued, "will inscribe over its altar, as its sole qualification for membership the Saviour's condensed statement of the substance of both law and Gospel, 'Thou shalt love the Lord thy God with all thy heart, and with all thy soul, and with all thy mind, and thy neighbor as thyself,' that church will I join with all my heart and all my soul." The books which he chiefly read, in his leisure hours were, the Bible, Shakspeare, the peasant poet of Scotland, with whom his sympathies were very acute, and those peculiar off-shoots of American wit, of which Orpheus

C. Kerr, Artemas Ward, and Doesticks are types. I frequently saw all these books in his hands, during a voyage of three days upon the Potomac, when the party consisted only of the President and his family, the Secretary of War and his aid and myself.

The ten months which divide the fall of Fort Donelson, (February 16th, 1862,) from the battle of Fredericksburg, (December 13th, 1862,) constitute the depressing era of military uncertainty. Administrative ability, executive resolution and hardihood, were never more impressively displayed than during this disheartening period, but in spite of it, inconstant victory seems to vibrate between the hostile banners.

The encouraging results of Iuka and Corinth, and the opening of the Upper Mississippi, inspire the national heart with new confidence in the protection of Heaven and in the heroism of our western soldiers. Brave old Farragut earns the grade of Admiral, and the soubriquet of Salamander, by leading his thundering Armada, through the *feu d' enfer*, which belched from Fort Phillip on the right, and Fort Jackson on the left, and the martial and financial heart of rebellion in the Southwest, is palsied when the guns of his fleet sweep the streets of New Orleans, and the Tamer of Cities hangs up its scalp in his wigwam. War surges and resurges over the

44

devoted plains of Missouri and Arkansas. The Peninsula Campaign, with its chequered fortunes, alternately excites exultation and wailing, but its final failure plants in the National heart the seeds of despair, while the whirlwind which devours the army of Pope, constrains us to doubt the justice of God. The victories of South Mountain and Antietam, fairly costing their weight in gore, and turning to ashes in our grasp, failed to reanimate our hopes, while Pittsburg Landing and Shiloh, are more than counterpoised by the heart rending butchery of Fredericksburg.

The progress of MR. LINCOLN's mind from his plan of colonizing the slave, and after that was abandoned, to compensated liberation, and from this expedient to unconditional emancipation, is analogous to the deliberate advance, which I have already detailed, from a conservative to a thorough going policy, in the prosecution of the war. Unlike the first, however, in these last transitions he meets with no resistence from the philanthropies of his nature, but encouraged and stimulated by the complete accord of emotion and reason. To be self-willed in a revolutionary crisis, and to exclaim "Justice shall be omnipotent though the Heavens fall," are unquestionably sublime manifestations, but in such imminent peril, it is rather the sublimity of madness than

of wisdom. I can not withhold my tribute of gratitude and admiration, to the caution and address,
with which MR. LINCOLN has felt his way, timeing his
march to the beat of the popular heart, and answer-
ing no requisitions of the popular will until it was
thoroughly mature and unmistakably pronounced.
He had settled the principle upon which emancipation is defended, and was unquestionably ripe for it
himself, when he first resolved to exercise the belligerent rights which belonged to the Government, in
time of war, but he was deterred from exercising
the right of liberation, from the apprehension of a
counter revolution in the North, and that his fears
were not entirely groundless, that remarkable political revulsion, in the fall elections which immediately
follow his preliminary proclamation, abundantly
demonstrates. When, however, his convictions of
the justice of emancipation were enforced, by the
logic of continued failure, and by the incisive reasoning of the enemy's unyielding sword, he was led
up, in spite of his fears, to the height of that trans-
cendent Edict, which constitutes his strongest claim
upon universal and unending gratitude and remembrance. He assumed the Presidential chair, with a
solemn disavowal of any constitutional right to inter-
fere with slavery in the States, and if they had continued faithful to the Constitution, their cherished

barbarity, condemned as it was by all his moral
instincts, would have been safe in the inviolable
sanctity of his oath. But when they appealed to
War, and voluntarily renounced the safeguards of
the Constitution, they instantly handed over the
abhorrence of civilization to uncovenanted mercy,
and disengaged two belligerent rights, one of which
is fatal to it, if slaves are *chattels*, and the other fatal
if slaves are *men*. By the most meliorated construc-
tion of the international code, the private property
of an enemy on the land is still liable to capture,
under circumstances constituting a necessity, of which
the conqueror is the sole judge ; while the old and
austere authority of Vattel establishes the indisputa-
ble right in one belligerent, to break the chains of
any oppressed people which the other belligerent is
depriving of liberty, for the purpose of completing
and ennobling victory. Of these weapons, MR. LIN-
COLN chose the first, which is called military necessity. The conditional proclamation was for some
time postponed, awaiting the impending engagement
in Maryland, and was finally promulged only five
days after Antietam. MR. LINCOLN required that the
military urgency upon which it was based, should
not only be plausible, but real and imperious, and
it is now well understood that if victory had perched
more signally on our banners, and Lee's army had

been more thoroughly crippled and demoralized in that battle, the proclamation which restores to millions of living men, and to unborn generations, the rights of manhood, would have been postponed to an indefinite future.

Are we not here able to interpret and explain one of those purposes which are sometimes called mysterious and inscrutable ? I can almost see a mighty arm, stretching out of the unfathomable blue, hastening the fugitive in his flight, holding back the feet of the pursuer, and arresting the waves of destruction which are pouring upon the dismayed and broken ranks, that the abyss which is yawning for the mightiest of slavery's hosts, may not swallow up the elect of liberty and the redemption of a long suffering race. Assembled here, to-day, to devoutly recognize that Providence, which guided the great liberator, "by ways which he knew not and by paths which were not known," may we not all of us, without a discordant voice, and with the hope that his own ransomed spirit is not unconscious of the oblation, unite in the invocation which closes the imperishable manifesto, "UPON THIS ACT, BELIEVED TO BE AN ACT OF JUSTICE WARRANTED BY THE CONSTITUTION UPON MILITARY NECESSITY, I INVOKE THE CONSIDERATE JUDGMENT OF MANKIND AND THE GRACIOUS FAVOR OF ALMIGHTY GOD."

The definitive proclamation of emancipation was

promulged on the first of January, 1863, and it seems instantly to have been visited with that "gracions favor" which it so reverently implores. From that eventful date Federal ascendency flows surely and steadily on to the capture of Richmond and the surrender of Lee. Reverses and checks, it is true, intervene, but they are only eddies in the Amazon. During these twenty-seven controlling months of the war, into which more general engagements were crowded, than into any equal period of the world's history, the loss of but one, attests the advent of higher inspiration and divine re-enforcement to our struggling cause. The ink with which the proclamation is written is scarcely dry upon the parchment, before the decisive victory of Murfreesboro expels invasion from imperiled Tennessee. On the nation's birthday which next follows it, propitious heaven almost visibly intervened, by breaking the last barrier which prevents the loyal father of waters, from flowing free and unobstructed through the divided rebellion; and by sweeping back, from the bristling hills of Gettysburg, the army of the alien on its last desperate raid into the bosom of the North. Away up in mid air, on the cloud capped crests of the south-eastern Alleghanies, there is the roar and lurid flame of battle, as if the pent up fires of the cavernous earth were bursting from their thunder-riven summits, while down, down in the deep valley, it seems as if the elements of nature were battering chasms and pathways through their granite foundations. The gates of Georgia yield to the flushed battalions of the Cumberland, and from the Altamaha to the Cape Fear, three great states of the Confederacy soon "feel the victor's tread and know the conquered knee." Hood is hurled, by his infatuated Chieftain, against the battlements of Nashville only to be dashed back broken and destroyed. The vale of the Shenandoah is swept by the besom, and scourged by the wrath of Sheridan. Over the forest which sweeps from the Rapidan to the James, there hangs, in early Spring time, a dark and portentous cloud; the Wilderness is red as if untimely Autumn had purpled its foliage. We dimly hear, far in its resounding depths, that awe-inspiring roll, that sharp suggestive rattle which forewarns and terrifies nations, and ever and anon a woe-begone messenger, such as

> "Drew Priam's curtain at the dead of night
> And told him half his Troy was burned"—

breaks from the sequestered thicket, with a tantalizing tale, of the fierce, sanguinary, but indecisive shock and recoil of embattled hosts. What weeks of heart-rending suspense! But finally, from the Saturnalia of death and butchery long rampant in its sombre and haunted recesses, he of the iron will and inflexible tenacity, at length emerges in the resplendent robes of Victory, and day after day for persistent months, unmoved by clamor, undismayed by failure, unwearied by resistance, slowly tightens an irresistible coil, round the wailing Capital of sin, until faint and gasping, it falls into the arms of a negro brigade. City after city, harbor after harbor succumbs. The coast is hermetically sealed from Norfolk to Galveston, and the magazines and arsenals of England and France no longer pour their strengthening tides into the decaying veins of the worn out Confederacy. Sheridan rolls up the Confederate right like a scroll and hangs on its flying flank with the scent of a hound and the snap of a terrier. Lee surrenders his decimated horde, and over the old endeared, precious inheritance from the Rappahannock to the Sabine, up flies the banner, down droops the rag.

ABRAHAM LINCOLN's work was finished, when unheralded and almost unattended, leading his little son by the hand, he walks into the streets of humiliated Richmond. If upon that auspicious morn, the crowning benediction had descended upon him, he might have well wished to die. What more could he ask for on earth? Assailed by the strongest conspiracy

that ever threatened a nation's life, after a four years'
struggle, his triumph over it was complete and over-
whelming, conquering liberty for a class and national
existence for a people. Was not this honor enough
for one man? He had survived ridicule, he had out-
lived detraction and abuse, he had secured the com-
mendation of the world for purity of purpose, constancy in disaster, clemency in triumph, and the
praise even of his armed foes, for gentleness and
mercy. In times more troubled, he had administered
Government with more ability than Cavour, and War
with more success than Napoleon the Third. He
had paled the glory of Hastings in preserving an
empire, and had earned comparison with Hampden
for self-command and rectitude of intention, while as
the emancipator of a race, he stood alone in solitary
glory, without a rival and without a parallel. If
fame had approached him with the laurels of a conqueror, if power had offered him a sceptre, and
ambition a crown, he would have scorned them all.
He asked from man, he asked from God but one
culminating boon, peace, peace on the bloody waters
and the blighted shore.

Alas! such an enviable consummation to his career
was denied. There are mysterious conferences of
suspicious and guilt-laden men, ominous flittings of a
bat-like flock from Washington to Richmond, and

from Richmond to Canada, midnight interviews, lurking spies, correspondence in cypher; a conspiracy against his life has long been maturing, in minds capable of such things, and finally the day is named, the place is appointed, and the parts of the bloody drama all distributed. On the evening of the 14th of April, 1865, at Ford's theatre in the City of Washington, the trigger of a pistol is pulled by a sneaking murderer who had crept up behind him all unwarned, and the report resounds through the startled assembly. From the private box which the PRESIDENT was known to occupy, an excited wretch, with a swart visage torn and convulsed by every passion, leaps upon the stage where he had last played the bloodthirsty Apostate, and brandishing a dagger in his outstretched hand, and exclaiming " sic semper tyrannis," vanished into night and darkness, leaving behind him horror, terror and woe. The nation stands aghast! the crime of the Dark Ages has entered our History—stealthy assassination has broken the sacred succession of the people's anointed—the life of the best beloved of Presidents is oozing from a murderous wound—the soul of Abraham Lincoln is transferred from Earth to Heaven.

Whether the Confederate Government is legally guilty of MR. LINCOLN's murder, is a question yet to be determined, but of one thing we are sure, that no crime is too bad, too bold, too infamous, too execrable, for that state of society which was willing to unchain the fiends of war, to incarnadine sea and land, to immolate a Republic that is to the victims of misgovernment the only pledge of ransom, and to the victimizer the only warrant of retribution, to bore into Pandemonium itself and surge this consecrated earth with its sulphurous seas of flame, that it might continue to batten forever on slavery, and perpetuate eternally "such abominations as are buried under the waters of the Dead Sea." Assassination belongs to the same ruffian family of crime in which that society exulted previous to the war, and to the same degree of infernal turpitude with those which it had encouraged and applauded, during its prosecution. Without compunction or hesitation, it could coolly plot to pile hecatomb upon hecatomb of victims, infancy and age, guilt and innocence, in one smouldering heap, by the midnight conflagration of our crowded metropolis. It could stealthily conduct the infection of a devouring pestilence, as electricity by the wires, into the healthy atmosphere of the North, that all who breathed it might die. It could deliberately compose the fiendish plan, and day after day, hour after hour, composedly weigh and measure out to helpless prisoners, the precise ration which was sure to produce their slow starvation. What a burlesque to see such a society shrink back affrighted and horror struck, at shooting one Abolitionist in the head and stabbing another in the heart! In the name of Christianity it justifies Human Bondage, in the name of the Constitution it justifies its over- throw, in the name of Chivalry it justifies the Bloodhound and the Barracoon, why not in the name of Patriotism justify Assassination, and ap- prove and ratify the hired murderer's lying epi- taph upon himself when with the price of blood in his pocket·he says, "tell my mother I died for my country." What a record of lawlessness and infamy has slavery written for itself from Mr. Lincoln's elec- tion to his death! Appealing to the Ballot, it abjures the verdict of the people, appealing to Pub- lic Opinion, it defies the decree of the civilized world, appealing to Arms, it tramples on the Code of War and summons Starvation, the Torch, and the Plague, to aid the impotency of its sword. Too wicked to live in peace, too weak to succeed in war, too enraged to accept defeat, too corrupt to die with honor, too putrid to rise again, it gathers up its expiring strength to strike an assassin's blow that it might die as it had lived, violating every law, human and divine, and accursed by God and man.

"Useless, useless," said the dying Thug, as his shrieking ghost fled from the angry earth to the vengeful skies. Yes, yes, crime always fails in its purpose, assassination is everlastingly a blunder. Cæsar is assassinated, and imperial sway emerges in full armed despotism from his tomb—Henry the Fourth is assassinated, but the edict of Nantes survives for nearly a century the dagger of Ravaillac, and religious toleration is invigorated by its blow—William the Silent is assassinated, but the republic of the Netherlands breaks the double fetters of superstition and tyranny, and expands into a great and flourishing commonwealth—Buckingham is assassinated, but Protestant Rochelle is soon delivered up to the vengeance of Richelieu—Capo D'Istria is assassinated, but the European dynasties control the policy and elect the kings of Greece—LINCOLN is assassinated, but the branded confederacy cowers beneath the maledictions of the civilized world, and onward, onward, roll the mighty wheels of victory and vengeance. "Useless," and didst thou dream, impious malefactor, that it was in the power of thy puny arm to reach the great life of our virtuous DELIVERER ? He lives! he lives! he lives to-day, in his imperishable example, in his recorded words of wisdom, in his great maxims of liberty and enfranchisement. The good never die ; to them belongs a double immortality, they perish not upon the earth, and they exist forever in heaven. The good of the present live in the future, as the good of the past are here with us and in us to-day. The great primeval law-giver, entombed for forty centuries in that unknown grave, in an obscure vale of Moab, to-day legislates in your halls of State, and preaches on your Sabbath in all your synagogues. Salem's royal singer indites our liturgies and leads our worship. Socrates questions Atheists in these streets. Phidias sculptures the friezes of Christian temples—the desecrated tongue of mangled Tully arraigns our Catalines—against the Philip of to-day the dead Demosthenes thunders—the dead Leonidas guards the gates of every empire which wrestles for its sovereignty—the dead Justinian issues in your courts the living mandates of the law—the dead Martin Luther issues from your press the living oracles of God—the dead Napoleon still sways France from that silent throne in the Invalides—the dead George Washington held together through wrangling decades this brotherhood of States, and the dead ABRAHAM LINCOLN will peal the clarion of beleaguered nations and marshal and beckon on the wavering battle line of liberty, till the last generation of man—

> " Shall creation's death behold
> As Adam saw her prime."

His fame will grow brighter and grander, as it descends the ages, and posterity will regard him as the incarnation of democracy, in its pure childhood, as the embodiment of those ideas of universal emancipation, which were the glory of its youthful epoch. In remote futurity, as far removed from us as we are from the Chaldeans, when the massive walls of our Capitol shall no more exist than the palace of Nebuchadnezzar, and all that is mortal in our civilization and polity shall live only in memory, and when the ingenuous child, gazing adown the dark infinity of time, will be obliged to ask "where is the nineteenth century?" " There, there," the sage will reply, " where you see that full orbed and splendid HESPERUS of the West." When the race shall have finally climbed to the lofty table land of UNIVERSAL BROTHERHOOD, to which it is inevitably destined by the paramount law of its own development, and shall turn backward its wistful eyes for those who have led its weary pilgrimage, through passes the most perilous, and over wastes the most disheartening, they will instinctively seek the uncourtly figure of that forest born LIBERATOR, who, by one glorious edict restored to humanity all the divine equalities enfeoffed upon it, when of one blood all the children of men were made, and thus incorporated into harmonious fraternity all the estranged and repellant complexions of mankind. With reverent and grateful hearts they will pour their choicest frankincense at the feet,

5

crown with unfading amaranth the brow, and by eulogy, statue, column and obelisk, and every aid to enduring remembrance, transmit to new and ever rising futurities, the irradiated name of the first President of the regenerated Republic, that Martyr to Liberty and Law, whom, on this shore and border of Time's immensity we deplore to-day, ABRAHAM LINCOLN of Illinois.

CPSIA information can be obtained
at www.ICGtesting.com
Printed in the USA
BVHW041442091118
532665BV00007B/27/P